# BIG ARMS

## "basics, 'breviated and best"

---

**WARNING**

This course stresses the importance of using proper technique and safety when using a bodybuilding or strength training program. Check with your health practitioner to ensure that it's appropriate for you to follow such a program. Follow the instructions carefully. Neither the authors nor CS Publishing Ltd. will be responsible for any physical injury that may result from following the routines and advice given in this course.

---

**BIG ARMS** Copyright © 1993 by Brooks D. Kubik and Stuart McRobert. All rights reserved. Cover illustration work by Stephen Wedan, Copyright © 1990.

Published by CS Publishing Ltd., P.O. Box 8186, Nicosia – CYPRUS.

Printed in Cyprus by Zavallis Litho Ltd.

# WHERE WE STAND

We're dedicated to providing the most consistent, practical, hype-free and undiluted source of training information for typical, drug-free bodybuilders. (While this arm course is primarily aimed at bodybuilders, our publications also provide instruction for function-first strength athletes.) Though our focus is always upon training methods that work for genetically-typical people, the instruction we promote works even better for those blessed with better-than-average genetics.

The reality of bodybuilding needs to be embossed on every training publication. Spectacular development (that of professional and top amateur contestants) can only belong to a minuscule minority of bodybuilders. Such development necessitates extraordinary genetics *plus* heavy and long-term use of bodybuilding drugs. This is the reality, no matter how persuasive some advertising copy, article, book or word-of-mouth statements to the contrary may be. Also, while usually portrayed, either explicitly or implicitly, as being the epitome of health and well being, and worthy of emulation, such development – due to drugs and the extreme dietary measures needed for the "ripped" condition – is the antithesis of health.

The irony of bodybuilding is that the training methods generally promoted to the masses only deliver the goods for those who are *extraordinarily* blessed genetically, or for those who use drugs to compensate for genetic shortcomings. Advice that emanates from the drug-assisted and/or the genetically gifted almost always has nothing, and I mean *NOTHING*, to do with what's needed by typical, drug-free bodybuilders. Any training advice taken from that source usually causes training "suicide" for the hard gainer.

This training course gives you the "taste" of what effective training methods are about. Yes they fly in the face of conventional gym instruction, but they need to because conventional training instruction has an appalling failure rate. Have a look around any typical gym. Take away the drug users and the few who can grow muscle virtually no matter how they train, and you'll be left with no big and strong bodybuilders in almost every gym you visit.

Conventional bodybuilding is distinguished by the almost universal application of training methods that produce little or no gains for most users. Most bodybuilders train for years with only minimal results. They waste their time with puny poundages and useless programs. Our publications will teach you how to become one of bodybuilding's exceptions: a success story.

## Our publications are about:

1. More practical, instruction-dense, time-proven training advice for typical, drug-free people than can be found anywhere else.

2. Radical opinions telling you what you need to hear, not just what you may want to hear.

3. Training methods that actually work without great genetics and without drug assistance; methods that will get you on the road towards a 400-pound squat, a 300 bench press and a 500 deadlift, and even *beyond* if you have the motivation, persistence, body structure and patience.

4. Training routines that rely mostly upon traditional and commonly available equipment.

5. Putting the non-competitive huge majority of bodybuilders first, not the minority of genetically-gifted and drug-using competitive bodybuilders.

6. Step-by-step training programs for beginners, intermediates and advanced bodybuilders, plus challenging but realistic targets.

7. Material written by typical, drug-free people, and instruction that keeps in mind that few people are free of demanding work and family responsibilities – most people just can't adopt a live-in-the-gym devotion to training.

Through HARDGAINER (a magazine published by CS Publishing Ltd., since July 1989) there are consistent, bimonthly reminders of how to keep on the training "straight and narrow," with a variety of authors providing their views.

Bodybuilding isn't a mysterious, complicated, time consuming and expensive activity like many would have you believe. You can achieve miracles with the very basic equipment, only a few hours of training each week, and without needing to buy any food supplements. The essence of our message is "basics, 'breviated and best," which is what this course for bigger arms is all about. Actually, "basics and 'breviated" isn't only "best," it's the *only* way to go for most drug-free bodybuilders.

Getting substantially bigger and stronger is about using progressive poundages – a bit more, a bit more again, and then a bit more again and again and again... while *always* maintaining good exercise form. (Religiously keep written records of your workouts, to keep track of your poundages, reps and sets.) The exercises that matter the most are the big, basic "building" exercises, i.e., the multi-joint "compound" exercises, not the little isolation exercises. Conventional bodybuilding has mesmerized and distracted people with inordinate amounts of writing and attention being given to marginal, incidental or irrelevant concerns. All the attention in the world to the variety of different training modalities, different rep cadences, different set and rep schemes, "scientific" and "physiological" rationales, isolation or "detail" exercises, "new" exercises, supplement "discoveries," personalities, contests, videos, training camps and seminars count for *absolutely nothing* unless you're adding more and more iron to the bar, *in good form*, as the months and years go by. If you're not, then, like hundreds of thousands of others, you're just getting more and more knowledgeable about everything and anything except that which will actually make you grow bigger and stronger.

Once you're beyond the beginner stage of bodybuilding, the bedrock of progressive poundages is the cycling of training intensity. *Always* trying to add poundage to your limit working poundages *isn't* the way to go. Instead, train in periods (cycles) where you cut back at the beginning of each cycle (to get a "running start") and take several weeks – adding 5-10 pounds per week to each lift – until getting to 10-15 pounds of the best poundages you were using before starting the new cycle, for whatever reps you're using. Then, get hold of a selection of little discs of varying small weights: half pound, one pound, 100 grams, 250 grams and 500 grams, or use improvised weights of light collars, large metal washers or even taping small pieces of iron onto bigger plates. Use these to notch up your exercise weights so slightly that you don't feel you're adding weight.

Take a further few weeks to get to your most recent best working poundages. Once there, keep adding a very small dose of iron every week to each exercise. You can build strength for perhaps months at a time if you keep adding a tiny dose of iron each week. However, if you get impatient and keep adding 5 pounds a week, you will "kill" the "gaining momentum" because you'll be adding iron at a rate in excess of your body's ability to build strength. Slowly, steadily, surely and safely is the way to go. Once the poundage gains finally "dry up," end the cycle, layoff for 7-10 days, cut back your poundages, perhaps change something in your routine for the sake of change and variety, and then build up again. Each cycle should have you starting a little higher than did the previous one, and have you finishing at higher poundages than did the previous one. (There are many ways to cycle training intensity. Extensive detail on it can be found in BRAWN.)

Part of the reality message we promote is believable measurements. Much fiction is presented as fact in the bodybuilding world, including absurd measurement claims by some of the most genetically gifted and "juiced" top achievers. For typical, drug-free bodybuilders, here are the reality-land measurements you should be looking at. A muscular and flexed 16" upper arm is very good, 17" is astonishing, and over 17" is fantastic.

Don't for a moment belittle a 17" arm. Such an arm, in muscular condition, looks *enormous* on a man with average bone structure. If you're a typical trainee, but build 17" arms, everyone who sees you will swear your arms measure 18" or better.

Read – Understand – Apply – Persist – Achieve

Stuart McRobert
Director
CS Publishing Ltd.

You may be wondering where the photographs of massive arms, long lists of different arm exercises, arresting anatomical drawings and exploits of the top physiques are. Those things are not here because, while they certainly attract readers and grab their attention, they too often cause confusion and distraction while not providing practical and useful training instruction for typical, non-competitive bodybuilders. Millions of underdeveloped people have become encyclopedias of bodybuilding-related information, but they remain underdeveloped because they simply don't know how to train themselves.

CS Publishing Ltd. provides a fundamentally different perspective so you can still read whatever you want to in order to be in touch with what's happening in the bodybuilding world, but do this while learning from our publications how actually to train yourself. After all, developing an impressive physique of your own (by drug-free standards) is far more satisfying and enjoyable than is looking at, and reading of, the spectacular achievements of others.

# BUILDING 16" ARMS

**Introduction by Stuart McRobert**: For those of you who already have muscular arms of 16" or better, turn to the second (advanced) part of this course. Few people have muscular 16" arms, so most of you will have to focus upon building them before qualifying for the advanced course.

Flynn's Gym is an iron monster's dream come true. The dumbbells go up to 200 pounds. The gym boasts eight full-sized power racks, and four platforms for deadlifts and Olympic lifting. It holds twenty Olympic barbell sets. There are eight heavy-duty competition-style bench press benches, two chinning bars, two pairs of dipping bars, four trap bars, a standing calf machine, a seated calf machine, four overhead pulleys for lat work, two gripping machines, some thick bars and deadlift handles, and nothing else.

Flynn has a theory about that. He says that if you cram a gym with non-essential pieces of equipment all you do is encourage people to avoid the result-producing basic movements in favor of lighter, easier exercises.

"If I were to put a hack machine in here," he said, "some poor misguided soul would probably use it. Same with a leg extension unit. And I bet he wouldn't even do squats. Imagine what a travesty that would be. I would feel so guilty."

Flynn's training philosophy is nowhere more evident than in the special training courses he drops on beginners who want to bomb and blitz a particular body part to Herculean proportions. Take the Flynn's Gym arm routine, for example.

About one year ago a scrawny kid came into the gym, signed up for a one year's membership, and proceeded to try to curl himself to death. He had one of those space-age, high-tech training programs that so appeals to teenagers. Where he found it no one ever knew. The routine was endorsed by a popular bodybuilding star, who at 5'8" and 225 pounds claimed it had built his arms to 24" in record time. I think he also said he could curl 400 pounds for 22 reps and do lying tricep extensions with 450 pounds.

## THE WRONG WAY

The kid trained his arms five days a week. He did 58 sets for the triceps and 72 for the biceps. He threw in 27 sets of forearm work to finish things off. He used tri-sets, supersets, giant sets, pre-exhaustion, compounds, forced reps, and negatives.

When he first joined the gym, Flynn asked the kid if he would like to try "a good, time-tested program that some of our other members have had success with." The kid politely declined, stating that he had a special, "advanced" training program.

After watching his antics for six weeks, Flynn tried again, at the end of the kid's two-hour bicep and tricep marathon. "How's the arm routine going, Champ?"

"I was going to ask you about that," said the kid. "You know, this doesn't seem to be working like Mr. Everything said it would."

No kidding," thought Flynn. He sipped his coffee and didn't say a word.

"Maybe I need to try something new."

"Sometimes that's a good idea," said Flynn. He took another long drink of coffee. "A new routine can work wonders when you're in a rut."

"Maybe I should add ten more sets of multi-angular blitz curls," suggested the kid, "supersetted with inverted low-pulley tricep extensions."

## THE RIGHT WAY

Flynn fortified himself with another swig of coffee, counted to ten (silently), took a deep breath and plunged into the eye of the storm.

"How would you like to try the Flynn's Gym arm specialization routine?" he asked.

"You have a special routine?"

"Sure," said Flynn. "A secret program – only for members of Flynn's Gym."

That caught the kid's attention fast.

"Now then," continued Flynn, this may seem a little different to what you're used to. Even the champ who endorsed your current training program might not know about it. But we've had lots of success with it around here."

"Tell me about it," said the kid, looking at Flynn the way my dogs look at me when I'm halfway through a steak sandwich and starting to slow down.

### The kid's background

Flynn began by getting some basic information. He asked the kid how much he could bench press.

"About 120 pounds for five reps – but I don't bench too often, because I don't want my chest and shoulders to take away from my arm size."

Flynn asked the kid how much he could squat and deadlift.

"I never do those. Mr. Everything said they aren't important. He never does them. And besides, too much leg and back work might tire me out for curls and kickbacks."

Flynn asked about the kid's diet. The kid lived almost exclusively on some high-tech supplement full of anabolic-metabolic-pseudo-opti-neuro-granulated-retractable-amino-activators. The kid explained that you had to eat right if you wanted to look like a champ."

"Yeah, that's probably true," Flynn noted, keeping a straight face. "Did you say 'champ' or was it 'chump'?"

### The program's background

Flynn sent the kid off to take a shower and change, and sat down to write out a workout program. The kid was back fifteen minutes later to pick up his program. He read it from top to bottom, stopped and read it again.

"When do I do curls? And where's the tricep work?"

Luckily, Flynn had anticipated the questions and had an answer ready.

"This is the latest Bulgarian training program. It's based on a scientific principle called neuro-bio-optimization: NBO. Many of the top champs swear by it."

"But why don't I do any curls?"

"Molecular refraction," Flynn answered. "Anyone can do curls by doing curls, but only a champ builds his arms molecularly."

The psycho-babble convinced the kid to give the program a try, although he seemed awfully concerned when he learned he'd only be lifting two times a week.

### The first stage's workouts

"This program is serious stuff,' said Flynn. "So you need to start slow and easy. You'll do only three exercises on Monday: squats, bench presses and pulldowns. On Friday, you'll do deadlifts, shrugs, chins, and close-grip benches with a 16" grip.

Your goal is to get strong – two or three times stronger than you are now. To do that, you need to limit the amount of work you do and focus only on the basic exercises. They're the strength developers.

Use the 5 x 5 system on each exercise. Do 5 reps with a light weight for a warmup. Add weight and do a second warmup. Then add more weight and do 3 sets of 5 reps with your 'working weight.' Later in the program, the working sets will be as heavy as you can manage. Start out easy and add weight to the bar every week. The idea is to do a month or so of relatively light workouts – break-in training, we call it – then work hard for two months. The break-in period is critical, because it helps avoid injuries *and* because it helps create what Stuart McRobert calls a 'gaining momentum.' If you start out heavy you'll bog down halfway through the program.

Look, you said you bench 120 pounds for five reps, right? Here's how your training cycle should look over the next twelve weeks." Flynn started writing out the cycle on a sheet of pale green paper:

| Week # | | | |
|---|---|---|---|
| 1 | 60x5 | 80x5 | 100x3x5 (3 sets of 5) |
| 2 | 70x5 | 90x5 | 105x3x5 |
| 3 | 75x5 | 95x5 | 110x3x5 |
| 4 | 80x5 | 100x5 | 115x3x5 |
| 5 | 85x5 | 105x5 | 120x3x5 |
| 6 | 90x5 | 110x5 | 125x3x5 |
| 7 | 90x5 | 115x5 | 130x3x5 |
| 8 | 90x5 | 120x5 | 135x3x5 |
| 9 | 90x5 | 120x5 | 140x3x5 |
| 10 | 90x5 | 120x5 | 142x3x5 |
| 11 | 90x5 | 120x5 | 144x3x5 |
| 12 | 90x5 | 120x5 | 146x3x5 |
| 13 | 90x5 | 120x5 | 148x3x5 |

"Shoot for a similar poundage progression on all of your exercises, of course. Note though, an intermediate or advanced guy can't handle weekly increments like you can, as a beginner."

### The new diet

The kid changed his eating habits dramatically. At Flynn's direction he buried the super supplement in his backyard. We wondered if it would kill the crabgrass. (It did.) The only pill he swallowed was a multi-vitamin/mineral tablet, and only one a day. The rest of his diet consisted of good, solid food: eggs, milk, cheese, meat, fish, macaroni, bread, potatoes, vegetables and fruit. He ate four or five big meals every day. Whenever he felt hungry he took a bite of something solid. Whenever he ate he washed it down with a cup or two of milk.

"Should everyone eat like the kid is now?" I asked Flynn.

"No. This diet is only for the real skinny guys, particularly the youngsters," Flynn replied. "The over-30 crowd should stick to three good, solid meals a day. The main point is to eat a good, healthy diet and get your nutrition from food instead of supplements. As your training gets heavier and harder, you need to increase your food intake somewhat to be sure you have the extra supplies your growing body needs."

Three months later, the kid had added 30 pounds to his bench press, 40 to his squats and 45 to his deadlift. He was ten pounds heavier, all of it muscle. Flynn told him he was doing well and it was time to move to the second stage of the program after taking a ten-day layoff.

### The second stage

"Dr. Slicktork, an exercise physiologist from California, has just come up with a new training secret. He calls it 'power training,'" Flynn told the kid. "All the really big guys swear by it."

"Will I do curls and tricep extensions now?" the kid quizzed.

"No. We need to keep optimizing the metabolic flushing factors. Dr. Slicktork swears by it."

"Does Dr. Slicktork have big arms?"

"Bigger than anyone who ever followed your old routine. Honest."

Once again, the kid bought into the double-talk. Flynn put him on a three-day-per-week schedule, using the 5 x 5 system on each major exercise:

*Monday*
1. Squat (to parallel): 5 x 5
2. Bench press (26" grip): 5 x 5
3. Pulldown (to the chest): 5 x 5
4. Seated press behind neck: 5 x 5
5. Standing calf raise: 2 x 20 (same weight for both sets
6. Crunch sit-up: 1 x 40-50

*Wednesday*
1. Incline press ($45^0$ incline): 5 x 5
2. One-arm dumbbell row: 5 x 5 (5 sets for each arm)
3. Barbell shrug: 5 x 5
4. Crunch sit-up: 1 x 40-50
5. Side bend: 1 x 30-40 (each side)

*Friday*
1. Squat (to parallel): 5 x 5
2. Close-grip bench (16" grip): 5 x 5
3. Bent-legged deadlift: 5 x 5
4. Seated calf raise: 2 x 20 (same weight for both sets)
5. Crunch sit-up: 2 x 40-50

Flynn told the kid that since Friday would be his second squat workout of the week, he must only use 70-80% of the weight used on Monday, and take it easy.

The kid finished each workout by hanging from a chinning bar for as long as possible, a great exercise for the forearms and grip, and a good way to work the kinks out of your back after a heavy workout.

Three months after starting the second stage, the kid had packed on an additional eight pounds of muscle and was starting to handle some fairly decent training poundages. Flynn decided it was time to move him up to level three in the training program, following a ten-day layoff.

### The third stage

"This is the new blitz-pump system that all the guys in Florida are using," Flynn explained. "It's the latest thing."

"Will I do any curls?" asked the kid.

"Not yet," answered Flynn. "We still need to vascularize the lobotomy."

"Yeah, I think I heard about that."

Flynn put the kid back on a two-day-per-week training program – a different routine for each day. The kid used the 5 x 6 system, i.e., five sets of six reps, using three progressively heavier warmup sets and two heavy sets on each major exercise:

*Monday*
1. Squat (to parallel): 5 x 6
2. Parallel bar dip: 5 x 6
3. Chin (palms facing away, medium grip): 5 x 6
4. Shrug: 5 x 6
5. Standing calf raise: 4 x 10-15
6. Crunch sit-up: 1 x 40-50

*Friday*
1. Deadlift (stiff-legged or bent-legged, straight bar or trap bar): 5 x 6
2. Bench press: 5 x 6
3. Pulldown (to the chest): 5 x 6
4. Seated military press: 5 x 6
5. "Donkey" style or seated calf raise: 4 x 15-20
6. Crunch sit-up: 1 x 80-100 (no weight)

As in stage two, the kid ended each session by hanging from a chinning bar for as long as possible – except Flynn wrapped a towel around the bar to make it harder to hold onto. (The kid was starting to develop a darn good grip.)

Flynn knew that the kid had no shoulder problems and could do parallel bar dips safely as long as he did them carefully, under control and never overstretched. However, Flynn made the point that anyone who has had a shoulder injury should stay away from the parallel bar dip and substitute close-grip bench presses instead. Flynn also told the kid that while good technique instruction is available at Flynn's Gym, that isn't the case at most gyms. Therefore, bodybuilders need to get hold of a good book that goes into the details of technique on the big, basic lifts. Flynn recommended BRAWN.

The kid still followed the eating program Flynn had suggested. By this time, local food prices had gone up by about five percent – the law of supply and demand was in effect. The kid had discovered that food tastes better than supplements, even the ones with unpronounceable names.

At the end of the third stage's three months, the kid had packed on another seven pounds. His bench press was up a further 30 pounds, his squat by 40 and his deadlift by 40. By this time, he was starting to look reasonably big.

Flynn told the kid to go measure his arms. The kid – now 25 pounds of muscle heavier than ten months earlier – reported that they were 2½" bigger than before he started on Flynn's program.

"I'm not surprised," Flynn said. "The Flynn's Gym arm specialization routine always works."

*Flynn's afterthoughts*

This article accurately details one of the many successes of my arm specialization program. Here's the bottom line: no matter what you do, you won't get big arms until you pack on some bodyweight. To do that you need to train on the basics: squats, bench presses, deadlifts, rowing, chins, dips and presses, and keep adding weight to the bar – progressive poundages, always. Remember, "basics, 'breviated and best." If you must, throw in a few sets of regular barbell curls, but skip all the specialized tricep movements – they just wreck your elbows. Bench presses are the numero uno exercise for big triceps. Dips are also good, and overhead presses work the triceps real hard. So forget about the silly pumping and isolation exercises. Train hard and heavy, get lots of rest, eat plenty of good food and you'll build arms like a gorilla.

The real secret to specialization programs – at least for beginners and intermediates, and that means everyone with upper arms that measure under 16" – is this: don't bother with them. Just use the basic movements to build some basic muscle, focusing on slowly and steadily adding more and more weight to your exercises. You can't add 100 pounds to your squat and 80 pounds to your bench press without adding an inch or two to your arms (drug-free, I might add). On the other hand, you can't hope to benefit from a specialization program for a body part as small as the arms until you're already pretty big and strong. □

# ON TO 17" ARMS

**Introduction by Stuart McRobert**: Once you've built muscular 16" arms you can move into a different bracket of arm training. The following is more in line with the sort of specialization routine you may have anticipated before reading this course. While most conventional specialization programs are just plain foolish for typical, drug-free bodybuilders, their recommended timing is usually a joke because they try to put mass on a small area of the physique without there first being a lot of muscle throughout the body.

Don't follow the conventional, waste-your-time training route. Get yourself quite big and strong (into the 280-300 bench press, 370-400 squat and 450-500 deadlift category, or beyond) before you work into the sort of specialization program that follows. You must be able to make lifts around these numbers and measure 16" around the upper arms *now*, not in years gone by. I'm not saying that the above lifts will equate to a 16" arm for everyone. They won't. However, they are about right for many people and give you an idea of what you need to be lifting before you can consider yourself "advanced" by the standards of non-competitive bodybuilding.

Spud McFlannagin has been a member of Flynn's Gym from the day it opened. Spud is one of those lucky individuals who has achieved honor and distinction in two areas of endeavor worlds removed from one another. On the one hand, he owns the biggest pair of muscular arms that anyone at the gym has ever seen (other than Flynn's monstrous guns). Second, he's the only amateur beer maker in the city who can produce not only a potent but a palatable brew. In our neck of the woods, each and every bottle of Spud's Suds is an object of admiration and desire. Flynn, who usually receives a dozen or more bottles at Christmas, is generally reckoned as one of our luckiest citizens – at least for as long as the bottles last.

While the secret of Spud's Suds is known only to Spud, the program responsible for his incredible upper arm development is available to any advanced trainee at Flynn's Gym. Here then, in the words of the Master, is the special program responsible for the slabs of beef that McFlannagin calls arms.

## BEFORE YOU START

"Let's begin by talking about one basic point," Flynn told me. "And pay attention. This is critical."

"Advanced arm training is for *advanced* men only. This means guys who are approaching or have surpassed the 300-pound bench press, 400-pound squat and 500-pound deadlift that Stuart McRobert cites as reasonable goals for hard gainers. If you're not approaching these numbers, don't even think about a specialization program – not for the arms or any other body part. Regular training is not only all you need, but *exactly* what you need. If you try to get into any sort of specialization program too soon, all you will do is overtrain whatever body part you're exercising.

The high-tech, every-exercise-under-the-sun programs have caused incredible frustration by teaching novices with 11" arms to 'bomb and blitz' their biceps and triceps for 20 and 30 sets apiece. It makes my blood boil even to think about it. Advice like that would be considered criminal in any civilized society."

Flynn paused for a second, reached into his desk, and pulled out the floor plans for an addition to the gym he's thinking about building. He pointed to a small "X" along the back wall of the planned expansion.

"Do you know what that is?" he asked.

I shook my head.

"It's where I'm going to put two chutes that drop into an alligator pit. I think I'll start with ten or fifteen alligators. I won't feed them very much, so they will always be hungry. One chute will be for the muscle pumpers and another chute will be for the steroid brigade."

Looking at the big guy, I couldn't tell if he was joking. Muscle pumpers and steroid pushers are anathema to Flynn.

"Anyhow," Flynn continued, "this arm routine will do you no good unless you really are an advanced man. If you're not, keep following routines for the non-advanced man. Issues of HARDGAINER have routines for non-advanced guys as well as routines for advanced guys. Save this arm routine for when you're bigger and stronger."

## PHASE ONE

Flynn continued, "The routine has two phases. Phase one calls for three workouts a week, scheduled on Monday, Wednesday and Friday, or on Tuesday, Thursday and Saturday. You follow this routine for twelve weeks, no less and no longer, and then move to phase two of the program.

During this phase, or during *any* phase of *any* program for that matter, you must keep progressive poundages uppermost in your mind. You need to keep pushing to get stronger. Using the repetition ranges I'm going to give, you can't get stronger without getting bigger. And the other side of the coin is this – you can't get bigger without getting stronger. Remember that.

You see those little discs over there? We have about 50 of them scattered through the gym. They weigh one pound each. The members here use them to keep adding weight even when they feel they're already moving their top poundages. But remember to start out with relatively light weights – something like 70-80% of your max for the scheduled number of reps. Break into the program slowly. Pick up the intensity gradually so that you're not training all out until the fifth or sixth week of the program. If you push too hard too early in the cycle you'll stall out around week number five or six, and wind up with nothing to show for your efforts.

To be able to keep your training progressive, not only do you have to have intense workouts and sufficient recovery time between sessions, but you also need plenty of nutritious food. Remember, it's *food* your body needs to get bigger and stronger, not supplements, but be sure you're eating enough quantity to grow on. Simply put, eat as much as you can without making yourself fat."

*Mondays*

"On Monday, you do no direct arm work of any sort. Instead, you do a basic routine designed to trigger growth in all the major muscular structures of the body, including the arms. *The secret to getting results from an arm specialization routine is to combine your specialized arm work with a program that triggers overall body growth at the same time.* If you want to get bigger arms, you'd better plan to add five or ten pounds of muscle in the process.

Begin the Monday workout with two sets of eight reps in the parallel squat. These will be light, warmup sets. Do the first with a light weight, and the second with a little bit more. Don't go heavy in your warmups. Save your energy for the third set of squats. Once you hit the all-out part of the cycle, this third set will be 20 reps with as much weight as you can handle. Take several deep breaths between reps. That's right – just like the old-fashioned, heavy, 20-rep breathing squat program we use to turn mice into men.

Start out easy but aim for 150% of bodyweight on the 20-rep squats, and once you get to 150%, set your sights higher.

After the set of 20-rep squats, stagger over to a bench, lie down, and do one set of 30 breathing pullovers with a light weight. When I say light, I mean *light*. A 15-pound exercise bar is more than enough for a superman. If you use too much weight on the pullovers, your muscles will contract so tightly that you will not be able to expand your chest properly as you perform the movement. The thing to do is to emphasize deep breathing on the pullovers, not muscular contraction. And for goodness sake, do the exercise lying lengthwise along the bench – like you were doing bench presses – not with your butt off the bench and your body perpendicular to it. Doing pullovers in that style will overstretch, and weaken your abdominals.

After the squats and pullovers (once you're in the all-out part of the cycle), take a rest for 15-20 minutes. If you've done the squats correctly, you'll need the break. If you don't feel like you need the break, then you've not been squatting seriously. In fact, if you can move even a finger after five minutes, you've been loafing.

After your break, do five sets of six in the bench press and in pulldowns to the chest. *Don't* super set these movements. Do all of the bench presses and then all of the pulldowns. For each exercise, begin with a light warmup set, add weight, then do a medium-heavy warmup set, and then use your top weight for the day in the final three sets. Rest at least three, and better yet, five minutes before each heavy set.

Next, do one set of 20 or 30 reps in the crunch sit-up. Hold a heavy dumbbell across your chest. Do one or two sets for your calves and then finish off with some forearm work – hang from a chin bar until you drop off, or else squeeze a rubber ball non-stop for three minutes per hand or until your fingers turn blue."

## Wednesdays

During Flynn's lecture I was scribbling furiously and probably looked a little blue. Always thoughtful, Flynn reached into the refrigerator in the gym's office and pulled out his two remaining bottles of Spud's Suds. Eying one of the them regretfully, Flynn dutifully passed it across the table to me. We uncorked, raised our bottles in unison, took long swigs, sighed with contentment and continued with the Wednesday edition of phase one of the arm training program. [Flynn's note: "Kubik, like any other 'artist,' works better when properly fueled."]

"Wednesday's workout is nothing but arm work. This is a critical part of the program, but one that requires lots of caution. A workload like this is just what will get a novice or even an intermediate nowhere fast. It also can be a real crippler, even for an advanced man. You need to be sure to break into this program slowly and carefully. Go easy at first – use the first four weeks of the program as a breaking-in period. This is *critical*."

"Yeah," I interjected, "I remember how sore Spuds was when he failed to follow that excellent piece of advice. He couldn't straighten his arms for about a month."

"That's right," said Flynn. "And it was getting close to Christmas, and I was concerned that it might interrupt his holiday brewing. Good thing the ice, hot showers, massage and aspirin finally pulled him out of it. Do you remember the batch of suds he whipped up that year?" [Author's note: I did indeed.]

"But, hey, I guess we gotta get back to business," Flynn continued. "Begin the Wednesday workout with five sets of 6-8 reps in the seated dumbbell press. Do these on a real high incline bench if you have one available – use something like an 80 or 85-degree angle, and work into heavy weights for your working sets. Do simultaneous presses – none of this alternate arm stuff that you sometimes see. Or, if your prefer, do the seated press behind neck. Again, use an $80^0$ incline bench – it helps take pressure off of the lower back. Home-gym trainees in particular may find the barbell presses more convenient to do. On your presses, do one light warmup set, a heavier warmup set, and the heaviest possible weight for the final three sets – as long as you get four or more on your final set, the weight is okay. When you get to the point where you can do at least six reps on each of your working sets, add more weight.

Overhead pressing is a terrific exercise for the shoulders and triceps. That's right – I said it's a terrific triceps exercise. One thing you'll note about this arm routine is that it has no specialized movements for the triceps – no kickbacks, no lying tricep extensions, and no pushdowns. The reason is simple. You build the triceps by doing heavy pressing movements. The light work is window dressing. It doesn't build an ounce of muscle. Heavy overhead pressing is far superior for upper arm development. And using pressing movements to build the triceps will prevent those elbow injuries that seem to inevitably arise from the leverage movements.

The second exercise on the agenda for Wednesday is the barbell curl. Do five sets of 6-8 reps, using the same procedure as on the dumbbell presses. Use either a regular bar or an EZ curl bar, whichever you prefer. Do the exercise in good form – with deliberate exercise style - keeping the weight under control all the way up and all the way down. Take a deep breath before each rep. Flair the lats out and lock the elbows into the sides so that you can't move them when the reps get tough. And, as with the dumbbell presses, plan on working into *big* weights on this exercise. The barbell curl may be basic, but it's the best bicep exercise ever invented. Work at it hard, and you'll see what I mean.

The third exercise in the works on Wednesday is the close-grip bench press. Use a grip that puts your thumbs about 16" apart. Again, do five sets of 6-8 reps. If you have an EZ curl bar, you may wish to use it for this exercise. Together with the overhead presses, the close-grip bench press will be a killer for the triceps.

Finish the upper arm program with five sets of 6-8 reps in either the reverse barbell curl *or* the hammer curl with two heavy dumbbells. These will work the biceps and forearms from a different angle than does the barbell curl, and provide plenty of extra growth stimulation. If your second curling exercise of the day was a variation of the barbell curl, you would be working the same muscles you already hit with the barbell curls – a sure way to achieve nothing but overtraining. Doing reverse curls or hammer curls will avoid that problem because they have a different training effect than the barbell curl.

End with the same sort of forearm and grip work you performed on Monday. A nice set of muscular forearms increases the overall appearance of your arms enormously.

Train as heavy as possible after the first four weeks. Try to build up to some serious poundages: 70-75% of bodyweight for curls, bodyweight for presses, 125% of bodyweight for close-grips and 50% of bodyweight for reverse curls. There's no point in looking strong unless you *are* strong. But remember – work up gradually to big weights. Don't run out and try to curl a freight train your first day out."

By this time, the bottles of Spud's Suds were history. Flynn tossed me a can of a commercial brew – a lite beer, at that.

"I know, I know," he said. "But it's got less calories, and it's less filling too."

*Fridays*
Flynn continued with the Friday workout for phase one of the arm building program. "The first exercise is the lifter's choice," he said. "You can either do deadlifts, power cleans or stiff-legged deadlifts, whichever you more prefer doing. If you work the stiff-legged deadlifts, do four sets of eight reps. Start light and add weight on each set. Work up to your heaviest set of eight reps for the final set. If you do regular-style deadlifts or power cleans, do five sets of five, starting light and working up to your heaviest weight for one set of five reps. If you choose to do power cleans, be sure you know what good technique is and have *expert* coaching on hand. The power clean is technically more difficult a lift than are the deadlift variations. If you don't have expert coaching for the power clean, stick with a variation of the deadlift.

Next are shrugs, done with a barbell or trap bar, for four sets of eight reps. Again, start out with a light weight and add weight on each set. Work up to your heaviest set of eight reps for the final set.

The next exercise is parallel bar dips. Do these slowly and deliberately to avoid shoulder injuries. No bouncing – it's dangerous and non-productive. And be careful not to stretch too far at the bottom or you're asking for trouble. Do the first few reps very deliberately and take a few reps before you're doing the full range of dipping. Do one set of 30 reps. If you have a history of shoulder problems, you should skip the dips and substitute push-ups with your palms eight inches apart and your feet elevated to make the exercise more difficult. Another good alternative is bench dips – you know, the ones where you place two benches facing each other about four feet apart, put your feet on one and the heel of your palms on the another, and do a sort of reverse dipping motion with your body moving up and down between the two benches. You'll probably want to add a 50 or even a 100-pound plate for extra resistance – have a training partner place the plate across your upper thighs. [Author's note: *Don't* try using a stack of 25-pound plates – if they shift, as they will, you may have to say goodbye to your hopes of ever becoming a father.] Do one set of 30 or 40 reps. Work for a good burn in the triceps.

The next exercise is the close-grip chin. By a close grip, I mean that your hands are anywhere from 6-12 inches apart. Do the exercise with the palms supinated – in other words, facing you – as you do the exercise. Work slowly and deliberately and shoot for 15-30 reps, depending on your bodyweight. Lighter guys should shoot for 30 reps and heavier guys should aim for 15. When you meet your rep goal, tie 25 pounds of weight around your waist.

Finish the Friday routine with calf work for 2 or 3 sets, one set of 30 crunches – hold a dumbbell across your chest for extra resistance – and ten minutes of forearm work. Use a plate-loading grip machine, if one is available. If not, try pinch-grip work, wrist-roller work or any other of the many good gripping movements. While this arm program doesn't neglect the forearms, the focus is definitely upon the upper arms. When you want to get really serious about forearm and grip work, read Stuart McRobert's outstanding article in the March 1993 issue of HARDGAINER."

## PHASE TWO

"Stay on phase one of the program for twelve weeks. After that, move into phase two. Phase two lasts for only three weeks. During this three-week period you'll spend 95% of your time working your arms. The only exercises other than arm work that you'll perform will be five sets of squats on Friday of the first week, five sets of deadlifts on Friday of the following week, and another five sets of squats on Friday of the third week. For the squats and deadlifts, use the 5 × 6 system – two progressively heavier warmup sets, then three sets with as much weight as possible. For example, a guy who can squat 375 for 6 reps should do 250 × 6, 325 × 6 and 375 for 3 × 6. Rest five minutes between the heavy sets. Do either bent-legged or stiff-legged deadlifts, straight bar or trap bar, whichever you prefer. If you prefer power cleans to deadlifts, and know how to do them properly, that's fine.

The arm routine during phase two consists of the same exercises you used during the Wednesday program in phase one. On Monday and Friday, do the exact same program you used for Wednesday's workout during phase one. On Wednesday of phase two, however, change the sets and reps from five sets of 6-8 reps on each exercise to five sets of 8-12 reps. The first two sets will be progressively heavier warmups. On the final three, use as much weight as possible – try to handle 75-80% of your top weight for the same exercise when you only do 6-8 reps per set. In addition, conclude each workout on Wednesday with one set of the same dipping movement that you were using on Friday during phase one, and one set of close-grip chins. Do the maximum possible number of reps on the dips and chins. Don't add weight, just go for reps. Keep track of how many reps you do, and try to increase your record by two or three every Wednesday. But remember – good form is a must. Don't get sloppy."

## PUTTING IT ALL TOGETHER

"After three weeks on phase two," Flynn continued, "you take a complete break from all exercise for ten days, and then go back to phase one of the advanced program for another six weeks. Start light and take it easy for two weeks before getting into the heavy work again for four weeks. Follow this six-week period with a second go around on phase two of the program. Take another ten-day break and then go back to a more balanced training program, preferably one that emphasizes heavy squatting, benching and back work."

Flynn started to wrap the program up now. "If you're really interested in building big arms, do the full program once every year – twice through the two phases. You don't want to use it any more than that. If arms are your 'thing' and you go through the program once a year for two or three years, you'll end up with the biggest, strongest, most muscular arms that your body can carry. Don't forget, of course, to keep adding weight to your exercises. If you keep using the same poundages you'll keep having the same measurements."

"How many times has Spud used the arm routine?" I asked Flynn.

"Three times in the last five years, but then, Spud is an unusual case," Flynn answered. "He's the only man in history who simultaneously got the best possible and the worst possible results from an exercise program."

"What do you mean?" I asked.

"Spud's arms are huge," said Flynn. "And that's great. Problem is, his biceps are so big he can't bend his arms far enough to chug a bottle of suds. The guy brews the best bottled beer in the world but has to drink it with a soda straw!"

"That's incredible," I said, bending my own arms and trying to imagine not being able to drink from a beer bottle.

[Afterword by Flynn: "Gullible, isn't he? I love the guy. Send us a line at CS Publishing Ltd., and tell us how the routine works. And for goodness sake – subscribe to HARDGAINER and get a copy of BRAWN. Best darn investments you'll ever make!"]

## ADVANCED MAN'S PHASE ONE

*Monday*
1. Parallel squat: 1 x 8 light, 1 x 8 medium, 1 x 20 heavy
2. Breathing pullover: 1 x 30 using no more than a 15-pound bar
(Take a break for 15-20 minutes.)
3. Bench press: 1 x 6 light, 1 x 6 medium, 3 x 6 heavy
4. Pulldown: 1 x 6 light, 1 x 6 medium, 3 x 6 heavy
5. Crunch sit-up: 1 x 20-30
6. Calf work
7. Grip work

*Wednesday*
1. Overhead pressing (dumbbells or barbell) on an 80° incline bench if one is available: 1 x 6 light, 1 x 6 medium, 3 x 6-8 heavy
2. Barbell curl: 1 x 6 light, 1 x 6 medium, 3 x 6-8 heavy
3. Close-grip bench press (approx. 16" between thumbs): 1 x 6 light, 1 x 6 medium, 3 x 6-8 heavy
4. Reverse barbell curl or hammer curl: 1 x 6 light, 1 x 6 medium, 3 x 6-8 heavy
5. Grip work

*Friday*
1. a) Barbell or trap bar stiff-legged deadlift: 4 sets, starting light and working up to your heaviest set of 8 reps
  *or* b) Barbell or trap bar regular-style deadlift, or the power clean: 5 sets, starting light and working up to your heaviest weight for one set of 5 reps
2. Barbell or trap bar shrugs: 4 sets, starting light and working up to your heaviest set of 8 reps for the final set
3. Parallel bar dip: 1 x 30
  *or* elevated push-up: 1 x 30
  *or* bench dip: 1 x 30 or 40
4. Close-grip chin, hands 6-12" apart and facing you: 1 x 15-30
5. Calf work
6. Crunch sit-up: 1 x 30
7. Grip work

## ADVANCED MAN'S PHASE TWO

*Monday*
Same workout as on Wednesday during phase one (but with increasing poundages, of course)

*Wednesday*
Same workout as on Wednesday during phase one except change the set/rep scheme to 5 x 8-12, i.e., 1 x 8 light, 1 x 8 medium, 3 x 8-12 heavy
*plus*, a) one set to failure of the dipping movement used on Friday in phase one, without extra weight
  b) one set to failure of close-grip chins (as on Fridays in phase one) but without extra weight

*Friday*

Same workout as on Wednesday during phase one

*plus,* a) in weeks one and three, the squat for 2 x 6 warmups and then 3 x 6 heavy

b) in week two, the deadlift for 2 x 6 warmups and then 3 x 6 heavy, *or* power cleans for the same sets and reps

## TOTAL ADVANCED PROGRAM

1. *Phase one for 12 weeks (4 weeks of break-in training and 8 weeks heavy)*
2. *Phase two for 3 weeks*
3. *Ten-day layoff*
4. *Phase one for 6 weeks (2 weeks of break-in training and 4 weeks heavy)*
5. *Phase two for 3 weeks*
6. *Ten-day layoff followed by a return to a more balanced program*

When in the final stage of a cycle, regardless of whether you're using a non-advanced or advanced routine, you *must* pile on extra rest and sleep, and increase your intake of nutritious food. The final part of a cycle is the "new territory" stage, and you *must* supply the rest, sleep and food components in abundance if you're to make the best gains you can. Also, over the final weeks of a cycle, when you're training at your absolute hardest, you may feel your training routine has too many exercises in it, and you can't recuperate adequately. If so, then eliminate the calf, abdominal and even grip work for just these few weeks, and focus on the other exercises – the primary exercises for this training course.

If you've turned to the advanced routine before reading what went before it, this is an arm program for men who are already big and strong, i.e., guys who have arms measuring 16" or more, and who can bench press about 300 pounds, squat 400 pounds and deadlift 500 pounds. To get to this level, you *must* stick with programs like those described in the first part of this course. Save the advanced course for the time when you're truly advanced.

□

**No other consideration matters – be it coach, equipment, smart clothing, food, supplements, reading material or mental aid – until you've absorbed into your being, and put into practice, the absolute importance of progressive poundages, in good form, in the basic exercises.**

The appalling irony of modern bodybuilding is that the training methods appropriate to only a small minority of bodybuilders are given massive promotion, while the training methods most appropriate to the masses are largely hidden from the very people who need them the most.

The training methods detailed in this course have more than fifty years of verified results behind them.
The methods will work if you will.

No matter how hard the going gets, or how many setbacks or obstacles you have, keep at it. *Persist!*